John Ruskin

An illustrated life of John Ruskin

1819~1900

James S. Dearden

'The Author of "Modern Painters"', a portrait of John Ruskin painted in 1843 by George Richmond, whom Ruskin had first met two years earlier in Rome.

Contents

*British Library Cataloguing in Publication Data: Dearden, James S. (James Shackley).
John Ruskin: an illustrated life of John Ruskin, 1819–1900. – 3rd ed. – (Lifelines; 15)
1. Ruskin, John, 1819–1900 2. Authors, English – 19th century – Biography 3. Artists
– Great Britain – Biography 4. Critics – Great Britain – Biography 5. Social reformers
– Great Britain – Biography I. Title 828.8'09 ISBN-10 0 7478 0599 7.*

For
Sarah Washington

ACKNOWLEDGEMENTS
The images on pages 4, 5, 7, 8, 11, 12, 13 (upper), 14, 16, 17, 18, 21, 22, 24, 26,
27, 29, 32 (upper), 36, 38, 39, 40, 48, 59 and 63 are reproduced by courtesy of The
Ruskin Foundation; the image on page 19 by courtesy of the British Museum; that
on page 47 by courtesy of the Sheffield Galleries and Museums Trust; that on page
50 by courtesy of Whitelands College, and those on pages 37, 43 and 54 (upper) by
courtesy of Sarah Quill.

*Published in 2013 by Shire Publications Ltd, Midland House, West Way, Botley, Oxford
OX2 0PH. Website: www.shirebooks.co.uk Copyright © 1973 and 2004 by James S.
Dearden. First published by Shire 1973. Second edition, published by The Brantwood
Trust, 1981. Third edition, revised and updated and illustrated in colour, published by
Shire 2004. Reprinted in 2008, 2012 and 2013. Shire Library 511.
ISBN 978 0 74780 599 1.*
Printed in China through Worldprint Ltd.

John James Ruskin (John Ruskin's father) by George Watson, 1802.

The formative years

FAMILY BACKGROUND

John Ruskin was descended from London-Scottish ancestry. His grandfather, John Thomas Ruskin, was born in London in 1761. After early training as a vintner, he left London on the death of his father in 1780 and went to Edinburgh to become a grocer. His son, John James, was born in 1785, and at the age of sixteen was sent to London to begin a mercantile career.

John Thomas Ruskin was not a sound businessman. He was an extravagant man and six years after he had sent his son to London his own business failed and he became bankrupt. In the following year the Ruskins left Edinburgh and eventually settled in a rented house, Bowerswell, at Perth. By this time the household had been increased by the addition of Margaret Cock or Cox. She was the daughter of John Thomas's sister and had been sent from her home at Croydon to act as companion of John Thomas's wife.

Margaret Ruskin (John Ruskin's mother) by James Northcote, 1826.

Ruskin's birthplace, 54 Hunter Street, Brunswick Square, London, photographed on 1st January 1969 immediately before its demolition.

The two cousins, John James Ruskin and Margaret Cock, became attracted to each other and in 1809, at the respective ages of twenty-four and twenty-eight, they became engaged. John Thomas continued to lead a precarious existence until finally he became insane and in October 1817 he committed suicide at Bowerswell. In the previous month he had lost both his sister and his wife and it may have been this double tragedy which led to his own death. Soon after his father's death and nearly ten years after he had become engaged, John James Ruskin married Margaret Cock in February 1818.

In London, John James had profited from his training and after having several jobs he finally set up in business on his own account. While working for the firm of Gordon, Murphy he had met Pedro Domecq, whose family owned vineyards in Spain. In 1814 John James Ruskin, Pedro Domecq and Henry Telford established the firm of Ruskin, Telford & Domecq to import wines from Spain. John Ruskin was later to say of the firm that Telford supplied the initial capital, Domecq the wines, and his father the brains. John James was an astute businessman and the agency prospered. Soon they were importing more sherry from Jerez than any other shipper, a position which was to be maintained for many years. For most of his life John James ran the business alone, save for the help of his two clerks; Domecq had returned to Spain and was to die tragically in 1839. Telford, who had originally owned the offices in Billiter Street, took little active part in the work of the agency and died in 1859.

CHILDHOOD AND YOUTH

On their marriage in 1818 the Ruskins set up their home at 54 Hunter Street, Brunswick Square, a Georgian terraced house not far south of the future site of St Pancras station. Here on 8th February 1819 their only child, John, was born. From the first his parents foresaw a

career in the church for him. His mother particularly was deeply religious and most of his early reading was from the Bible and he was expected to commit large portions of it to memory. For weekday reading he was allowed a few other books. Few toys came his way and he recorded among his early pleasures counting the bricks on the façade of the house opposite, and examining the knots in the wooden floor 'with rapturous intervals of excitement during the filling of the water-cart, through its leathern pipe, from the dripping iron post at the pavement edge'. Ruskin recalled being taken to church as a small boy and how the horror of Sunday cast its gloom from Friday to Monday. However, what he heard there had its effect for he remembered delivering his own first sermon at home – 'People, be dood. If you are dood, Dod will love you. If you are not dood, Dod will not love you. People, be dood.'

The family remained at Hunter Street for only a few years, moving in 1823 to 28 Herne Hill, a much larger house in south London near the village of Camberwell. The house on Herne Hill was to remain their home for the next twenty years.

It was John James Ruskin's practice to act as his own business traveller and he made frequent journeys into the country to call on his customers. As soon as young John was old enough, the family went too. While John James made business visits in various areas, John, his mother and his nurse Anne Strachan would explore the region in which they were temporarily staying. John James's business often took him to many of the country's large houses and if the owners were away the butler was invariably persuaded to show the Ruskins around. Thus from an early age young Ruskin became familiar with different parts of Britain as well as with some of its art and architecture.

Ruskin enjoyed travelling by carriage and in 1875 he had this brougham, still preserved at Brantwood, specially built for a posting tour from London to Coniston.

These half business, half pleasure journeys were undertaken in Henry Telford's travelling carriage, which was loaned for the occasions. 'The old English chariot is the most luxurious of travelling carriages, for two persons, or even two persons and so much of third personage as I possessed at three years old. The one in question was hung high, so that we could see well over stone dykes and average hedges out of it... The "dickey" was thrown far back in Mr Telford's chariot, so as to give perfectly comfortable room for the legs (if one chose to travel outside on fine days)...'

One of these early tours, in 1824 when John was five and a half, took the Ruskins to Scotland to see their relatives and *en route* they spent a few days in the Lake District. The view of Derwentwater from Friar's Crag was to remain in John's mind for a long time and he referred to it in one of his books. 'The first thing which I remember, as an event in life, was being taken by my nurse to the brow of Friar's Crag on Derwent Water; the intense joy, mingled with awe, that I had in looking through the hollows in the mossy roots, over the crag into the dark lake, has ever associated itself more or less with all twining roots of trees ever since.'

By 1826 Ruskin's literary powers were beginning to develop and he was starting to write verse. From this year there are several poems recording another early visit to Scotland, written carefully in a hand imitative of printers' type. His first poem of any length (2310 lines) was entitled *Iteriad* and it recorded in considerable detail his three-and-a-half weeks visit to the Lake District in 1830. By now Ruskin was eleven and *Iteriad* shows that he had an inquiring mind, that his powers of observation were well developed, that he had a remarkable knowledge of Greek and Roman mythology and that he had begun to learn the classical languages. At this period John James was fostering his son's passion for writing verse by paying him at the rate of one penny for twenty lines, and hoping that, if after all he did not become a bishop, perhaps he might become a famous poet. So he must have been very pleased when his ten-year-old son's poem 'Lines Written at the Lakes in Cumberland – Derwentwater' was published in *The Spiritual Times* in 1829. Thus began a literary career that was to continue for a further sixty years.

By now Ruskin had also begun to draw. His earliest drawings, dating from 1827, were beautifully detailed little maps, done to teach himself geography. His first sketchbook, used about 1831–2, shows that he had also begun to draw from nature and take an active interest in the architecture of old buildings which the family saw on their travels. This skill was encouraged in 1831 when John James engaged the artist Charles Runciman to teach his son drawing; the lessons were to continue for several years.

As a thirteenth birthday present Henry Telford gave Ruskin a copy of Samuel Rogers's book *Italy*. The little vignette illustrations in the book by J. M. W. Turner greatly impressed Ruskin, who began to

Turner painted this vignette of the bridge at St Maurice for Rogers's 'Italy'. Ruskin later had William Ward make this copy of the original watercolour. Ruskin's landscape style in the 1830s was based on Turner.

An engraving of Samuel Prout's 'Ducal Palace, Venice', a drawing which later belonged to Ruskin. Ruskin's early architectural style was based on Prout.

imitate them and, as he wrote later, the book 'determined the main tenor of my life'. Soon afterwards the Ruskins bought a copy of Samuel Prout's portfolio of engravings *Sketches in Flanders and Germany*. So obvious was John's delight in both the subject and the style of Prout's architectural drawings that his mother suggested their next tour should be a real holiday. Accordingly on 11th May 1833 they embarked on their first large scale continental tour (Ruskin had first been abroad – to Paris – in 1825) following Prout's lead along the castles of the Rhine to the Alps. Henceforward Turner was their guide. John chronicled their tour in a long poem with illustrations in the styles of his idols, Prout and Turner.

One result of his 1833 industry and promise was that in the next year Ruskin began to take watercolour lessons from the president of the Society of Painters in Watercolours, A. V. Copley Fielding. The lessons continued for five years although Fielding's usual course of six lessons was calculated to produce an adequately skilled amateur in watercolours.

Ruskin's inquiring mind was now beginning to take an interest in geology and in 1834 he had three articles published in Loudon's *Magazine of Natural History* – 'Enquiries on the Causes of the Colours of the Water of the Rhine', 'Notes on the Perforation of a Leaden Pipe' and 'Facts and Considerations on the Strata of Mont Blanc, and Some Instances of Twisted Strata Observable in Switzerland' – and all of this at the age of fourteen!

Reputedly Ruskin's first continental drawing, 'Hotel de Ville, Cassel', 1833, drawn in his Prout style.

John Ruskin

In 1835 the Ruskins travelled on the Continent again on a tour lasting six months which took them through France, Switzerland and Italy. Ruskin kept a detailed geological diary for part of the tour, including daily readings on his cyanometer which recorded the colour of the sky, wrote a metrical journal of part of the tour and, as the present-day tourist would take photographs, Ruskin recorded what attracted his attention in an extensive series of pencil drawings. These drawings are important because they mark the blossoming of Ruskin the artist. The influences of Turner and Prout are very obvious. The architectural studies are detailed and precise, just like the engravings in *Flanders and Germany*, while the little landscapes might have been taken straight out of Rogers's *Italy*. In the evenings or in the winter following their return home Ruskin made finished drawings from many of his sketches, though they lose a lot in the re-drawing. And at least one of his sketches, 'Mount Pilate from the Lake of Lucerne', was used to make a watercolour drawing, employing all the tricks and mannerisms which Copley Fielding had taught him.

The advent into the Ruskin household in 1836 of Pedro Domecq's daughters brought a new influence into Ruskin's life and gave him a fresh subject for his poems, which by now were beginning to appear regularly in the annuals such as *The Keepsake and Friendship's Offering*. He fell in love, for the first time, with Adèle Domecq. At fifteen she

'Mount Pilate from the Lake of Lucerne', one of the extensive series of drawings that Ruskin made during his 1835 continental tour.

Above: The drawing of Mount Pilate was subsequently used as the basis for this dramatic watercolour. In it Ruskin has used all the tricks taught him by Copley Fielding, but, disheartened by his progress, he forsook watercolour for a while and returned to his pencil studies.

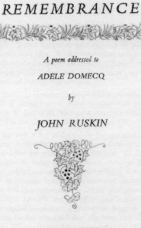

REMEMBRANCE

A poem addressed to

ADELE DOMECQ

by

JOHN RUSKIN

BEMBRIDGE
1970

'Remembrance', a poem addressed by John Ruskin to Adèle Domecq in 1837. This 1970 edition was printed by J. S. Dearden; the rosemary and vine illumination is by Margaret Adams.

13

John Ruskin

'Street Scene in Derby with All Saints Tower', one of Ruskin's fine 1837 architectural drawings.

was the eldest of the four unmarried daughters, 'a graceful, oval-faced blonde', who captivated Ruskin for a number of years. Both fathers would have been quite happy to have seen their children married, though they thought 'the time had not yet come to talk of such things'. But the puritanical Protestant Mrs Ruskin looked on the idea of her son marrying a Catholic Domecq as 'too monstrous to be possible... and too prepostrous even to be guarded against'. Finally Adèle was married in 1840 to the French Baron Duquesne.

For the most part Ruskin's early education was taken care of by his mother, though he read Latin and Greek under Dr Andrews and French grammar and Euclid under Mr Rowbotham. For two years he attended the Reverend Thomas Dale's school in Peckham and after he left in 1835 following an attack of pleurisy he attended a series of Dale's 1836 lectures at King's College, London. In 1837 John James Ruskin entered his son as a gentleman commoner at Christ Church, Oxford. But it was not just John who went to Oxford. The whole family went. Margaret Ruskin took lodgings in The High to be near her son during term and John James went there at the weekends from his London office or provincial tours. At Oxford Ruskin obtained the Newdigate Prize in 1839 for his poem *Salsette and Elephanta* and at the ensuing ceremony he and his father met Wordsworth, who was receiving an honorary degree. Ruskin took his BA degree in 1842 and MA in the following year. His career at this time was interrupted by recurring ill-health.

The summer tour of 1837 took the form of another visit to the Lake District, and it is chronicled by a fine series of architectural and landscape studies. For Ruskin it marked a milestone in his life, as it did with his immediate contemporary, Queen Victoria. They were born in the same year and she ascended the throne on 20th June 1837, the day before the Ruskins left London for the Lakes. During this tour, 'when I was eighteen, I felt', wrote Ruskin, 'for the last time, the pure childish love of nature which Wordsworth idly takes for an intimation of immortality... No boy could possibly have been more excited than I was by seeing Italy and the Alps; neither boy nor man ever knew better the difference between Cumberland cottage and Venetian palace, or a Cumberland stream and the Rhône:– my very knowledge of this difference will be found next year expressing itself in the first bit of promising literary work I ever did. . . The idea had come into my head in the summer of '37, and, I imagine, arose immediately out of my sense of the contrast between the cottages of Westmorland and those of Italy...'

Accordingly, the first part of *The Poetry of Architecture* appeared in the November 1837 issue of Loudon's *Architectural Magazine* and the fourteen parts continued until December 1838. Ruskin wrote under the pseudonym of 'Kata Phusin' – 'According to Nature'.

The 1838 tour began immediately after Ruskin had attended the Queen's coronation in Westminster Abbey on 28th June and again took the family to the Lakes. But this time they continued into Scotland for the main part of the holiday, which was to be a Sir Walter Scott pilgrimage. Scott was the Ruskin family's literary hero and they had always eagerly awaited the appearance of his new books. Ruskin had intended to write an article on Abbotsford to become the first in a new series in the *Architectural Magazine* called 'Homes of the Mighty' – but he was so disappointed in the house that the series never materialised. Instead he contented himself by collecting further material for *The Poetry of Architecture*, and making another fascinating series of drawings.

By this time Ruskin was beginning to develop a drawing style of his own. While it was still strongly affected by his heroes, his Proutesque architecture had begun to mellow and blend with his rather more detailed Turneresque landscapes. What little reputation Ruskin made for himself at Oxford was largely as a result of his skilful drawings, but this style was not to last much longer. Before the Ruskins went to Italy in 1840–1 John visited an exhibition of the drawings of David Roberts and *his*

Ruskin's drawing of the Trevi Fountain in Rome, 1841, showing the influence of David Roberts on his style.

Vesuvius in eruption, a study made by Ruskin during his 1841 visit to Naples.

influence may be traced in most of the drawings of this period.

The Italian tour of 1840–1 lasted for six months. They spent December in Rome, where Ruskin met George Richmond and Joseph Severn, who had been Keats's companion, before travelling as far south as Naples (9th January to 17th March). On their way home they spent ten days in Venice, where, on the first day, Ruskin wrote in his diary: 'Thank God I am here again! It is the Paradise of cities and there is a moon enough to make half the sanities of earth lunatic...' While in Venice he made many architectural observations in his diary, a foretaste of things to come.

About the time that he was twenty-one Ruskin's drawing style underwent a complete change. Throughout his youth all of his drawings had been done in imitation of other artists and he had been employing the mannerisms and tricks taught by his masters to 'make' pictures. But one day he was walking along the country road to Norwood when 'I noticed a bit of ivy round a thorn stem, which seemed, even to my critical judgement, not ill "composed"; and proceeded to make a light and shade pencil study of it in my grey-paper pocket book, carefully, as if it had been a bit of sculpture, liking it more and more as I drew. When it was done, I saw that I had virtually lost all my time since I

John Ruskin

This Venetian study of moonlight on the lagoon was made by Ruskin in 1849.

was twelve years old, because no one had ever told me to draw what was really there! All my time, I mean, given to drawing as an art; of course I had the records of places, but had never seen the beauty of anything, not even of a stone – much less of a leaf.'

This realisation was reinforced a few months later by a similar experience at Fontainebleau. 'I found myself lying on the bank of a cart-road in the sand, with no prospect whatever but a small aspen tree against the blue sky. Languidly, but not idly, I began to draw it; and as I drew the languour passed away: the beautiful lines insisted on being traced, without weariness. More and more beautiful they became, as each rose out of the rest, and took its place in the air. With wonder increasing every instant, I knew that they "composed" themselves, by finer laws than any known to man. At last the tree was there, and everything that I had thought before about trees, nowhere.'

The road to fame

TURNER

For a number of years John James Ruskin had been a modest picture collector and had gathered works by Copley Fielding, Cox, Holland, Roberts, and quite a few by Prout, whose work had been so admired by his son. These had all been moderately priced pictures but as he grew more prosperous he began to pay more for his pictures. The first really expensive one, Holland's view of Venice at 25 guineas, came in 1836, to be followed in the next year by two of J. F. Lewis's at £25 and £50.

John James shared his son's admiration for the work of J. M. W. Turner, the greatest contemporary master, and at the beginning of 1839 began to collect his pictures. The first was *Richmond, Surrey* at 55 guineas, to be followed at the end of the same year by *Gosport* at 60 guineas. Urged

Richmond Bridge, Surrey, c.1831; the foundation of Ruskin's extensive Turner collection.

J. M. W. Turner's self-portrait, c.1793. This was bequeathed to Ruskin in 1854 by Mrs Danby, Turner's housekeeper.

on by his son's admiration for the artist, John James rapidly became a dedicated Turner collector, spending £1232 15s on fifteen more pictures in the next five years. But the money was well invested for one of the purchases brought about an introduction to the master himself. 'I found him a somewhat eccentric, keen-mannered, matter-of-fact English-minded gentleman; good natured evidently, bad-tempered evidently, hating humbug of all sorts, shrewd, perhaps a little selfish, highly intellectual.' Turner was not an easy man to get on with but the acquaintance ripened as far as the eccentric artist's habits would permit. The Ruskins entertained regularly and frequently there were authors and artists of repute at their table. Turner was an occasional guest on a New Year's Day or at John's annual birthday dinners.

Both father and son continued to collect Turner's pictures for many years, building up one of the finest private collections, and in their generosity they also presented important collections of Turners to both Oxford and Cambridge. On Turner's death in 1851 Ruskin was appointed his executor and spent a considerable amount of time and money on framing and cataloguing the 19,000 sketches which the artist had left to the nation.

DEFENCE OF TURNER

An article by the Reverend John Eagles, a minor author and artist, in *Blackwood's Magazine* in 1836, criticising and condemning a number of Turner's paintings then on exhibition, annoyed the seventeen-year-old Ruskin and he composed a long article in reply, praising and defending his hero. For various reasons the article was never submitted for publication; however, it was an important milestone in Ruskin's career for it provided the germ of the book which was to bring him fame. In 1842 the *Literary Gazette* carried further criticism and Ruskin devoted the winter of that year to writing a book in Turner's defence. *Modern Painters: their superiority in the art of Landscape Painting to all the Ancient Masters proved by examples of the True, the Beautiful, and the Intellectual, from the Works of Modern Artists, especially from those of J. M. W. Turner, Esq., RA.,* was published on 5th April 1843 under the pseudonym of 'A Graduate of Oxford'.

Ruskin set himself an ambitious plan for *Modern Painters* but to a certain extent he was ill-equipped for the task in hand. On most of his trips abroad he had been observing landscape rather than studying pictures, though of course he had visited a number of galleries. In England, although he knew a group of Turner drawings intimately, there were many pictures by Turner which he had never seen. Most of the pictures which he referred to in the book were either in the National Gallery or his neighbouring Dulwich Gallery. The plan of the book was to test the value of Turner's work by its qualities of power, truth, beauty and intellectual content. Despite its various shortcomings it is a masterpiece of English prose and inescapably a work of genius. With

Ruskin's study of 'Mountain Rock and Alpine Rose' was made during the continental tour of 1844.

This study of the central detail of Tintoretto's 'Crucifixion' was made by Ruskin in the Scuola di San Rocco, Venice, in 1845.

its dramatic word pictures, balanced arguments and analyses of natural forms, *Modern Painters* was something completely new in art criticism, and was acknowledged as such by artists, critics and reviewers almost without exception. Ruskin had firmly laid the foundations on which his power as a writer on art was to be based for the next forty years.

Eager to continue his writing on art – he wished to expand his discussion of 'Truth' with further illustrations of mountain form, trees and skies in a second volume – the Ruskins went to Switzerland in 1844 so that John could begin by studying botany and geology at Chamouni. Thus the tour continued, ending with an examination of the Old Masters in Paris. The next year saw Ruskin on tour again studying Old Masters, now for the first time without his parents. It was in Venice during this 1845 tour that Ruskin discovered the Tintoretto paintings in the Scuola di San Rocco. His letters to his father had been including league tables of Italian artists, but Ruskin was bowled over by the Tintorettos and he told his father: 'I have had a draught of pictures today enough to drown me. I was never so utterly crushed to the earth before any human intellect as I was today, before Tintoret.... put him in the school of Art at the top, top, top of everything...'

In the following year the second volume of *Modern Painters* was published. The work continued intermittently until 1860, when the fifth and final volume of the book was published. Ruskin's own

Ruskin etched the plates of his drawings for the first edition of 'The Seven Lamps of Architecture', 1849. This image was printed from one of his plates.

experience and faculties developed as the book grew and one can find him contradicting in later volumes things he had said in earlier ones. But *Modern Painters* is not only a study of ancient and modern art, it is a profound piece of philosophy dealing with most of the vital problems of life.

ART, ARCHITECTURE AND MARRIAGE

During the seventeen years spanned by the publication of Modern Painters Ruskin continued his writing in other spheres. The early 1840s saw the end of his serious poetry writing; later he was reviewing such books as Lord Lindsay's Christian Art and Eastlake's History of Oil Painting and he also contributed notes on painting and architecture to Murray's *Handbook for Travellers in Northern Italy*. In 1846 he began planning *The Seven Lamps of Architecture*, a book in praise of the Gothic architecture which Ruskin loved. It was published in 1849 and was the first to be illustrated by his own drawings. Most of the fourteen illustrations were printed from plates which he had etched himself. The book was generally well received and Charlotte Brontë declared that the book was 'no lamps at all, but a new constellation'.

THE KING OF THE GOLDEN RIVER;
OR,
THE BLACK BROTHERS.

CHAPTER I.

How the Agricutural System of the Black Brothers was interfered with by South-West Wind, Esquire.

A secluded and mountainous part of Stiria there was, in old time, a valley of the most surprising and luxuriant fertility. It was surrounded, on all sides, by steep and rocky mountains, rising into peaks, which were always covered with snow, and from

The opening page of 'The King of the Golden River', first published in 1851.

23

Effie Gray, to whom Ruskin was married from 1848 to 1854.

Between the planning and the publication of *Seven Lamps* a change was to take place in Ruskin's private life. He had first met Effie Gray, daughter of his father's friend George Gray, who by now lived at Bowerswell, in 1840. She spent a few days with the Ruskins while on her way to school near Stratford-upon-Avon. In the following year he had written a fairy story – *The King of the Golden River* – for her. In 1848 the two were married at Bowerswell; but Ruskin's parents did not attend the wedding, perhaps because of the house's unhappy memories.

Two pages from 'House Book I', 1849, one of the extensive series of 'Stones of Venice' notebooks. Kenneth Clark said that if Venice were to be destroyed it would almost be possible to rebuild it using Ruskin's notebooks.

The opening page of the Kelmscott Press edition of 'The Nature of Gothic', 1892.

The pattern of Ruskin's life did not change a great deal as a result of his marriage. The tours abroad, both with and without the elder Ruskins, continued, while Ruskin assembled material for his various books. For his wife's sake he did become more involved in fashionable life, though he did not enjoy it. The winter of 1849 and the ten months spanning 1851 and 1852 were spent living in Venice, for Ruskin was working on another book – *The Stones of Venice*. The first volume appeared in 1851 and volumes two and three came two years later. In Venice Ruskin undertook the monumental task of drawing and measuring almost every feature of architectural interest and importance. He made literally thousands of sketches and filled page after page with detailed notes and measurements. In Venice, as elsewhere in Europe, the restorers were at work and Ruskin felt the need to record the old buildings before they were, to his mind, destroyed. But *The Stones of Venice* is no mere guide to the city. It is an artistic and architectural history of the Venetian civilisation examining the faith and nature of the people through an examination of the work of their craftsmen and artists. The chapter on 'The Nature of Gothic' particularly increased the number of Ruskin's disciples in Britain. William Morris, who chose the chapter in 1892 to be printed by his Kelmscott Press, considered it 'one of the most important things written by the author, and in future days will be considered as one of the very few necessary and inevitable utterances of the century. . . it seemed to point out a new road on which the world should travel.'

John Ruskin

MORE MODERN PAINTERS

In 1849 the new Pre-Raphaelite Brotherhood, Holman Hunt, John Everett Millais and Dante Gabriel Rossetti, first exhibited their new style of pictures at the Royal Academy. Holman Hunt had read *Modern Painters* I and found much therein which he believed. Both Ruskin and the Brotherhood believed that art should be an exact imitation of nature and that art and literature should be closely allied. The Pre-Raphaelites, whose paintings were so different to those being exhibited alongside them, did not achieve any measure of success. In 1850 Ruskin had seen Millais's 'Christ in the House of His Parents' but was not impressed by it and *The Times* critic violently attacked Holman Hunt's and Millais's pictures in the 1851 Academy exhibition. Millais asked Coventry Patmore, a mutual friend, to get Ruskin to come to their aid. Ruskin saw a need to defend the young artists in their pursuit of Truth and wrote two letters to *The Times* in their defence. He also added a note commending the high degree of finish of Pre-Raphaelite pictures to the new edition of *Modern Painters* which he was preparing. This

Ruskin's study of gneiss rock and the torrent at Glenfinlas, 1853.

Ruskin's lectures were illustrated by large diagrams. This diagram of a Venetian arch was prepared at Glenfinlas for his Edinburgh lectures, in 1853, by Ruskin and Millais; the gilding was done by Effie.

championship did much to bring the new school of art to the public's notice and also paved the way for the success of the Brotherhood.

Ruskin's public-spirited help of the Pre-Raphaelites was to lead to domestic trouble. It was natural that he should meet the artists themselves, and when in 1853 Ruskin and his wife were planning a holiday in Scotland they invited Millais and his brother to join them. In the winter of 1853 Ruskin was to begin a new phase in his career by delivering a series of lectures in Edinburgh on architecture and painting. Ruskin's marriage was not a success. The couple were incompatible – parental interference had not helped matters – and their relationship had declined. At Glenfinlas in the summer of 1853, while Millais painted Ruskin's portrait and Ruskin worked on his lecture notes, Effie and Millais fell in love. In the following year she left Ruskin and their marriage was annulled on the grounds that it had never been consummated.

27

Broadening interests

WORKING MEN'S COLLEGE

The lectures which Ruskin delivered in Edinburgh during the winter of 1853 marked the beginning of a whole new phase in his career and opened up a much wider audience than had been available to him through his written word. In addition, his interests were broadening. He was beginning to notice the way in which people lived and the conditions of life in Victorian England.

Ruskin's views on the place of labour in the social and economic

John Ruskin at the age of thirty-seven, photographed in 1856 by William Jeffrey, who was in the art class at the Working Men's College, and subsequently a member of staff. This is the earliest photograph of Ruskin.

system were concentrated into the 'Nature of Gothic' chapter of *The Stones of Venice*. In 1854 the Reverend F. D. Maurice established the Working Men's College in London at 31 Red Lion Square. Ruskin heard of the venture through F. J. Furnivall and offered to take the art classes; soon he persuaded Dante Gabriel Rossetti to assist him with this. Ruskin's aim was not to make artists of the workmen attending his classes, but to make them better men – or in other words, to educate them. To this end he gave several hundred books from his own library to the college. No doubt Ruskin's interest in the early stages of the Red Lion Square venture helped towards its success. 'The Nature of Gothic' was reprinted as a pamphlet and distributed as a sort of manifesto to those attending the opening sessions; to the title of this reprint was added the subtitle, 'And herein of the True Function of the Workmen in Art'.

Several of the art class pupils were to continue their association with Ruskin. J. W. Bunney became a professional artist and executed many commissions for Ruskin in Venice; W. H. Hooper and Arthur Burgess became successful wood-engravers; William Ward became Ruskin's assistant teacher, an accomplished Turner copyist, and the agent for the sale of Ruskin's educational photographs. George Allen was to be closely associated with Ruskin for the rest of his life.

OXFORD

As early as 1847 Henry Acland, a friend from Ruskin's undergraduate days, had begun to press for the building of a Natural History Museum at Oxford. For some years discussion raged over whether Palladian or Gothic designs should be adopted. Eventually the Gothic party won

The Irish craftsman James O'Shea carving the 'Cat' window of the Oxford Museum in 1859. The window is the second on the right of the main entrance, above the ground-floor window designed by Ruskin. The university objected to cats and monkeys being used in the decoration and dismissed O'Shea, but not before he had begun a moulding of owls and parrots in honour of the members of Convocation.

and Benjamin Woodward's designs were selected. Ruskin was already known to Woodward because he had been persuaded by *The Seven Lamps* to adopt a Venetian Gothic style for his designs for the new library at Trinity College, Dublin. Rossetti introduced Ruskin to Woodward and Ruskin soon became involved with the team designing the ornamentation of the building; Ruskin was responsible for the design of at least one of the windows. At the same time Woodward was also building a Debating Hall for the Oxford Union. Again Ruskin took an active interest in the work and was pleased when Rossetti, Morris and other Pre-Raphaelites painted murals in the window bays.

At about the same time Ruskin became involved with the proposals for the building of the new National Gallery and in April 1857 was called to give evidence before the Royal Commission on the site. In concluding his evidence, the chairman asked Ruskin precisely what position he held. He explained that he was 'master of the Elementary and Landscape School of Drawing' at the Working Men's College and he added: 'My efforts are directed not to making a carpenter an artist, but to making him happier as a carpenter.'

ART CRITICISM.

ART CRITICISM AND PATRONAGE

In 1855 Ruskin began to write an annual series of pamphlets, *Notes on the Royal Academy*, in which he criticised selected pictures exhibited at the Academy each year. His criticism was taken seriously by artists and art-buying public alike and in 1856 a poem appeared in

Ruskin caricatured by Frederick Waddy as the Angel of Light flying over London dropping flowers of wisdom, labelled 'Ethics of the Dust', 'Stones of Venice', 'Seven Lamps of Architecture' and 'Modern Painters'. This caricature was published in 'Once a Week', 25th May 1872.

'Sir Galahad and the Holy Grail' by Elizabeth Siddal and Dante Gabriel Rossetti, one of the drawings given to Ruskin, presumably under the terms of his allowance in 1855–6.

Above left: George Allen's engraving of Purple Wreath-wort, or Marsh Orchis. Ruskin wrote: 'This plate is not only our best [in "Proserpina"] but is one of the finest things ever done on steel. It cannot be bettered.'

Punch by a 'Perfectly Furious Academician':

> I takes and paints,
> Hears no complaints,
> And sells before I'm dry;
> Till savage Ruskin
> He sticks his tusk in,
> Then nobody will buy.

N.B. – confound Ruskin; only that won't come into poetry – but it's true.

Ruskin's teaching at Red Lion Square continued and among the members of his class was a carpenter, George Allen, on whose life and career Ruskin was to have a profound effect. Ruskin persuaded Allen to become a wood-engraver and in succeeding years he engraved many of the blocks for Ruskin's books in addition to doing a lot of picture copying for him. This patronage of Allen was typical of the way in which Ruskin gave practical help to many artists. His guaranteeing to take from Elizabeth Siddal up to £200 worth of her drawings annually provided financial support for both her and Rossetti at a time when

31

Study from 'The Meeting of the Virgin and Elizabeth' by Tintoretto in the Scuola di San Rocco, Venice, by Edward Burne-Jones, copied for Ruskin in 1862. The Burne-Joneses travelled with Ruskin as his guests as far as Milan and then continued on their own to Verona, Padua and Venice, while Ruskin returned to Mornex.

Ruskin standing between William Bell Scott (left) and Dante Gabriel Rossetti (right), photographed in Rossetti's garden in 1863 by William Downey.

they needed it. Edward Burne-Jones and his wife, who became very close friends of Ruskin, were taken by him to Italy, ostensibly so that Burne-Jones could copy Old Masters for Ruskin, but really so that they could travel on the Continent, seeing art and architecture and developing Burne-Jones's powers as an artist.

POLITICAL ECONOMY

Ruskin's teaching at the Working Men's College was distilled into two books, *The Elements of Drawing* and *The Elements of Perspective*, manuals which are still sought by amateur artists today. Meanwhile his experiences with his drawing class led Ruskin to wider views of the nature of the arts and the duties of philanthropic effort and social economy, and he introduced some of his views on this into the third and fourth volumes of *Modern Painters* in 1856.

In the following year Ruskin was invited to lecture at Manchester during the period of the great Art Treasures Exhibition being held there. For some time he had been studying political economy but had found no answers in the current standard books on the subject to the questions he had put to himself. He wanted to know the best way of employing artists, of educating workmen, of regulating patronage. The acknowledged authorities had no answers to these problems so Ruskin put his own answers into his lectures, which considered art as wealth: the first lecture dealt with how to get it, and the second with how to use it. The lectures attracted considerable audiences and were printed as *The Political Economy of Art*. The exhibition authorities had selected as their motto 'A thing of beauty is a joy for ever', and when Ruskin reprinted his lectures in the 1880s he changed their title to *A Joy for Ever*, adding the subtitle *and its price in the market*.

In 1860 the fifth and final volume of *Modern Painters* was published and with it, at the age of forty-one, Ruskin concluded the first cycle of his life's work, from which he was popularly known as a writer on art. From now on his studies in art were to run in tandem with those in ethics.

UNTO THIS LAST

The publication of *Modern Painters V* in June 1860 was followed in August–November of the same year by what is probably Ruskin's greatest book, *Unto This Last*. A new literary periodical, the *Cornhill Magazine*, had been established in January with W. M. Thackeray as its editor. In the first year there were contributions by writers of the stature of Trollope (*Framley Parsonage*), Tennyson, Washington Irving,

The opening page of 'Unto This Last', 1860, in the 'Cornhill Magazine'.

Emily and Charlotte Brontë, Matthew Arnold, Thackeray and Elizabeth Browning. Ruskin contributed a short unsigned piece on 'Sir Joshua and Holbein' to the March issue and was invited to contribute a further series of papers. He took the opportunity to develop his views on political economy with *Unto This Last*, which began in the August issue.

Ruskin's pronouncements were considered dangerous heresies. For example, in the third paper he wrote: '... whereas it has long been known and declared that the poor have no right to the property of the rich, I wish it also to be known and declared that the rich have no right to the property of the poor.'

At this time, orthodox political economy gave the middle-class heirs of the

"Unto this Last."[*]

I.—THE ROOTS OF HONOUR.

AMONG the delusions which at different periods have possessed themselves of the minds of large masses of the human race, perhaps the most curious —certainly the least creditable—is the modern *soi-disant* science of political economy, based on the idea that an advantageous code of social action may be determined irrespectively of the influence of social affection.

Of course, as in the instances of alchemy, astrology, witchcraft, and other such popular creeds, political economy has a plausible idea at the root of it. "The social affections," says the economist, "are accidental and disturbing elements in human nature; but avarice and the desire of progress are constant elements. Let us eliminate the inconstants, and, considering the human being merely as a covetous machine, examine by what laws of labour, purchase, and sale, the greatest accumulative result in wealth is obtainable. Those laws once determined, it will be for each individual afterwards to introduce as much of the disturbing affectionate element as he chooses, and to determine for himself the result on the new conditions supposed."

This would be a perfectly logical and successful method of analysis, if the accidentals afterwards to be introduced were of the same nature as the powers first examined. Supposing a body in motion to be influenced by constant and inconstant forces, it is usually the simplest way of examining its course to trace it first under the persistent conditions, and afterwards introduce the causes of variation. But the disturbing elements in the social problem are not of the same nature as the constant ones; they alter the essence of the creature under examination the moment they are added; they operate, not mathematically, but chemically, introducing conditions which render all our previous knowledge unavailable. We made learned experiments upon pure nitrogen, and have convinced ourselves that it is a very manageable gas; but behold! the thing which we have practically to deal with is its chloride, and this, the moment we touch it on our established principles, sends us and our apparatus through the ceiling.

Observe, I neither impugn nor doubt the conclusions of the science, if its terms are accepted. I am simply uninterested in them, as I should be in those of a science of gymnastics which assumed that men had no skeletons. It might be shown, on that supposition, that it would be advantageous to roll the students up into pellets, flatten them into cakes, or

[*] "I will give unto this last, even as unto thee."—*Matt.* xx. 14.

8—2

Industrial Revolution a feeling of certainty and mystic protection, disguising the fact that a few people were making a lot of money by exploiting the poor. Ruskin's essays spread alarm and despondency among the middle classes and the reviewer in the *Manchester Examiner* wrote: 'If we do not crush him his wild words will touch the springs of action in some hearts and before we are aware, a moral floodgate may fly open and drown us all.' Another reviewer wrote: 'The series of papers in the *Cornhill Magazine*, throughout which Mr Ruskin laboured hard to destroy his reputation, were to our mind almost pitiful. It is no pleasure to see genius mistaking its power and rendering itself ridiculous.' One of Ruskin's few supporters was his friend Thomas Carlyle, who wrote to him: 'You go down through those poor unfortunate dismal-science people like a treble-X of Senna, Glauber and Alloes... I have read your paper with exhilaration...

such a thing flung suddenly into half a million dull British heads...
will do a great deal of good.'

Fearing for the very existence of his magazine if he allowed
Ruskin to continue, Thackeray asked him to conclude the series with
a fourth and final article. Ruskin continued in the same vein: '... in a
community regulated only by laws of demand and supply, but protected
from open violence, the persons who become rich are, generally
speaking, industrious, resolute, proud, covetous, prompt, methodical,
sensible, unimaginative, insensitive, and ignorant. The persons who
remain poor are the entirely foolish, the entirely wise, the idle, the
reckless, the humble, the thoughtful, the dull, the imaginative, the
sensitive and the well-informed, the improvident, the irregularly and
impulsively wicked, the clumsy knave, the open thief and the entirely
merciful, just and godly person.'

Towards the end of the same chapter we find one of Ruskin's greatest
passages: 'I desire, in closing this series of introductory papers, to
leave this one fact clearly stated. THERE IS NO WEALTH BUT LIFE.
Life, including all its powers of love, of joy and of admiration. That
country is the richest which nourishes the greatest number of noble
and happy human beings; that man is richest, who, having perfected
the functions of his own life to the utmost, has also the widest helpful
influence, both personal, and by means of his possessions, over the
lives of others.'

Two years later Ruskin published the four chapters of *Unto This Last*
in book form. Although at first the book was slow to sell, the sales
gradually increased and in 1877 a second edition of 2000 copies was
published, to be followed at regular intervals by others. By 1888 the
five reprints had added a further 9000 copies to the original edition.
Between 1862 and 1905 43,000 copies were printed and as well as
this there were many unauthorised American editions. In 1904 it was
translated into French, German and Italian; in 1918 into Japanese. In
1904 Mahatma Gandhi, the founder of modern India, read the book; it
had an immediate impact upon him. He translated it into the Gujarati
tongue and determined to change his way of life in the light of its
teaching. By the 1960s almost 30,000 copies of Gandhi's paraphrase had
been printed. In 1956 his paraphrase of *Unto This Last* was translated
back into English and between then and 1977 38,000 copies had been
printed. Ruskin considered *Unto This Last* his most important book
and said that if all his books were to be destroyed except one he hoped
that the one to be saved would be *Unto This Last*. In *Sesame and
Lilies*, two more Manchester lectures, he described *Unto This Last* as

John Ruskin's self-portrait, drawn about 1866.

'the only book, properly to be called a book, that I have ever yet written myself, the one that will stand, (if anything stand), surest and longest of all work of mine.'

Having lost his Cornhill platform, Ruskin found another in J. A. Froude's *Fraser's Magazine*. In 1862–3 four 'Essays on Political Economy' were published, and they were later reprinted in book form as Munera Pulveris. In these Ruskin described capitalism. 'Capitalists, when they do not know what to do with their money, persuade the peasants, in various countries, that the said peasants want guns to shoot each other with. The peasants accordingly borrow guns, out of the manufacture of which the capitalists get a percentage, and men of science much amusement and credit. Then the peasants shoot a certain number of each other, until they get tired; and burn each other's homes down in various places. Then they put the guns back into towers, arsenals, etc., in ornamental patterns; (and the victorious party also put some ragged flags in churches). And then the capitalists tax both, annually, ever afterwards, to pay interest on the loan of the guns and gunpowder. This is what capitalists call "knowing what to do with their money"; and what commercial men in general call "practical" as opposed to "sentimental" political economy.'

The practical crusade

NEW OPPORTUNITIES

John James Ruskin was always a little nervous of his son's publishing his radical views and theories. Perhaps they did not have his whole-hearted approval, or perhaps, good businessman that he was, he saw the linking of such heresies with the name of Ruskin as being bad for business. He was, after all, a careful man, even to the extent that when he was travelling he always took the second-best room at an inn, in case one of his customers should turn up and be prevented by his wine merchant from having the best! However, with the death of his father in 1864 Ruskin felt himself freer to continue his study of political economy and to develop his views still further with some practical experiments.

Beginning his career with John Thomas's debt of nearly £4000, John James had amassed a considerable fortune by the time of his death.

Ruskin was to inherit from his father £120,000 together with property worth a further £3000. The family picture collection was included in this figure at £10,000 but, as John James noted in his final summary of 'My entire property', 'Pictures as lately selling are worth £25,000'. This fortune was not the result of meanness for John James was always a generous supporter of both public and private charities. His donations

Three of Ruskin's houses were in Paradise Place, now called Garbutt Place, a turning off Paddington Street. The euphemistically named Paradise Place of 1864 must have seemed very different to today's Garbutt Place!

grew in direct proportion to his prosperity and his account books show that in the final four years of his life he donated nearly £12,000 to various charitable causes.

With his inheritance, Ruskin bought several houses in Marylebone and determined to try a practical philanthropic experiment. The houses were put into reasonable repair, the tenants were given a recreation ground, and fixity of tenure, and were charged what Ruskin considered a fair rent – a five per cent return on his capital as opposed to the twelve or more per cent which property of that sort generally returned. At first his experiment was ridiculed, but eventually many landlords practised what Ruskin had preached and shown would work.

Ruskin was helped in his experiment by Octavia Hill, one of his dedicated disciples. She first came under his spell through reading *Modern Painters*. She applied to Ruskin for instruction in art, and she did some copying work for him. They were also in regular contact when she became the secretary to the Working Men's College. Ruskin appointed her to manage his Marylebone property, a task which she undertook until 1881, when Ruskin sold the houses to her for £3500. Partly as a result of Ruskin's influence and teaching, Miss Hill was later to become one of the founders of the National Trust.

THE DESTITUTE AND CRIMINAL CLASSES

In 1868 Ruskin was asked to join a committee which was looking at how the 'improvident and more or less vicious persons' should be helped, 'for our neglect of the lower orders has reached a point at which it begins to bear its necessary fruit'. He spent two months of that year at Abbeville, then a beautiful medieval town, in northern

At Abbeville in 1868 Ruskin made an important series of drawings, including this study of St Wulfran's church towering behind the houses of the market place. With the exception of St Wulfran's, most of old Abbeville has now disappeared.

France. Much of his time was spent in making a series of fine drawings, particularly of the church of St Wulfran. But while at Abbeville he also wrote his *Notes on the General Principles of Employment for the Destitute and Criminal Classes* for circulation to the members of his committee. In it he suggested a number of occupations, many of which he was subsequently to put into practice himself elsewhere. Among these suggestions were road-making, 'bringing in waste land', harbour making, porterage (heavy goods to be moved by canal boats), repair of buildings, dressmaking and works of art ('Schools to be established on thoroughly sound principles of manufacture and use of materials') – work in pottery, metalwork, sculpture and decorative painting.

OXFORD AND CONISTON

On the death of J. J. Ruskin a young cousin, Joan Agnew, had come from Scotland to act as Margaret Ruskin's companion. In 1871 Joan was married to the watercolour artist Arthur Severn, son of Joseph Severn who had nursed John Keats in his last illness. In the summer of 1871 Ruskin was staying with the Severns at Matlock when he

The small cottage of Brantwood at Coniston. Ruskin made this sketch during his first visit to his house in September 1871 so that he could show Joan Severn his new home.

The Ruskins' home at 163 Denmark Hill, London SE5, to which they moved in 1842. Ruskin sold the house in 1872 following the death of his mother. This drawing was made by Arthur Severn to illustrate W. G. Collingwood's biography of Ruskin.

underwent a serious illness. For several weeks he was nursed by Joan until he was well enough to return home. During his illness he had said: 'I feel I should get better if only I could lie down in Coniston Water.' Soon after his return to London he learned that the republican wood-engraver W. J. Linton wished to sell Brantwood, his house at Coniston. Ruskin did not know the house, but he knew its situation overlooking the lake, and he immediately paid Linton his asking price of £1500 for the house and grounds.

At the end of the year Margaret Ruskin died. No. 163 Denmark Hill had been the Ruskins' home since they moved from Herne Hill in 1842. But now Ruskin had no need for the large house himself and the lease was sold. Ruskin had already given the lease of the Herne Hill house to the Severns as a wedding present and henceforward they kept rooms there available for Ruskin's use when he was in town. He had his own new home at Coniston and when he was not travelling on the Continent he was now spending a considerable amount of time at Oxford.

SLADE PROFESSOR

In 1869 the University of Oxford had appointed Ruskin its first Professor of Fine Art. He lectured at Oxford regularly until his final resignation from the chair in 1884. Most of his lectures over the years were printed in book form – *Lectures on Art, Ariadne Florentina* (lectures on wood and metal engraving), *Aratra Pentelici* (seven lectures on the elements of sculpture), *The Eagle's Nest* (ten lectures on the relation of natural science to art), *The Art of England* and *The Pleasures of England*. In 1871 he had established the Ruskin Drawing School at Oxford and endowed a Drawing Mastership there. Many of his own drawings and other pictures from his collection were given to the school to be teaching examples and he published catalogues of the collection.

At Oxford he continued his practical experiments by persuading a

Above: While restoration and building work was being carried out at Brantwood in 1872 Ruskin took a number of his friends to his favourite towns on the Continent. This photograph was taken in Venice. With Ruskin (left) are Mrs Hilliard, Joan Severn, Arthur Severn, Connie Hilliard and Albert Goodwin.

A caricature in the series 'Great Guns of Oxford', probably by Briton Riviere, 1874, depicts Ruskin, the Slade Professor, as the 'President of the Amateur Gardening Society'.

GREAT GUNS OF OXFORD . *President of the Amateur Landscape Gardening Society.*

John Ruskin

It was a popular outing to visit North Hinksey to watch Ruskin's undergraduate diggers at work. This drawing appeared in 'The Graphic' on 27th June 1874.

group of undergraduates to repair a short stretch of country road at North Hinksey. His gardener Downes supervised the work and among the talented group of Hinksey Diggers were A. E. Street, later to become a well-known architect; Arnold Toynbee, the sociologist and economist; Oscar Wilde, the wit and dramatist; W. H. Mallock, author of *The New Republic*; Alexander Wedderburn, later Queen's Council; and W. G. Collingwood, later Professor of Fine Art at Reading and a noted antiquarian. Ruskin entertained his diggers to breakfast before their work began and at one of these meals he expressed the wish to have Xenophon's *Economist* translated from the Greek. Wedderburn, and later Collingwood, volunteered to help with this task, and so began an association which was to continue for many years. Wedderburn was to become one of Ruskin's executors and was to collaborate with E. T. Cook in the monumental task of editing the thirty-nine volumes of the Library Edition of Ruskin's works. Collingwood was to devote himself to being Ruskin's secretary, editor of many of his books and his first biographer.

EXPERIMENTS AND PUBLISHING

Meanwhile other experiments had been undertaken in London. A corner shop and house, 29 Paddington Street, was leased near to the Marylebone property. Here it was Ruskin's intention to supply the poor of the neighbourhood with tea in packets as small as they chose to buy, without making an excessive profit on the subdivision of the chest, as was the usual practice. Two of Mrs Ruskin's old servants were engaged to run the shop and eventually they suggested that coffee and sugar should also be stocked. This meant that a man had also to be employed to help with the heavy lifting. It was part of Ruskin's policy that 'no advertisements, no self-recommendation, no catch-penny tricks of trade were allowed'. 'Mr Ruskin's Tea Shop' was only moderately successful. 'The result of this experiment has been my ascertaining that the poor only like to buy their tea where it is brilliantly lighted and eloquently ticketed and as I resolutely refuse to compete with my neighbouring tradesmen either in gas or rhetoric, the patient subdivision of my parcels by the two old servants of my mother's hitherto passes little recognised as an advantage by my uncalculating public...' Eventually Octavia Hill took over the management of the business.

Another experiment began about the same time as the opening of the tea shop. Ruskin was disgusted by the dirty condition of London's streets

'Mr Ruskin's Tea Shop' on the corner of Paddington Street and Chiltern Street still sells tea, augmented by much else.

and hoped, by example, to persuade the authorities to do something about the situation. He selected for his experiment an area a quarter of a mile square in Seven Dials and employed four youths, at a total of £2 12s weekly, to do the work under the supervision of David Downes. But the inhabitants considered the experiment a great joke and threw more rubbish into the streets as soon as Ruskin's men had swept them. After about a year the experiment was given up, 'partly because I chose too difficult a district to begin with... but chiefly because I could no more be on the spot myself, to give spirit to the men, when I left Denmark Hill for Coniston'.

Ruskin distrusted a commercial system based on unacknowledged profits and percentages. He disapproved of tradesmen making an excessive profit, or obtaining more business by being able to undercut their competitors' prices. He put his principle into practice in the field of bookselling by insisting that there should be a certain price fixed on each book and that the booksellers could add what percentage they pleased as their profit. But this meant that the public knew what profit the bookseller was taking, an arrangement which did not suit the trade, and for a while Ruskin's sales suffered in consequence.

However, when Ruskin planned his series of monthly letters 'to the Workmen and Labourers of Great Britain', called *Fors Clavigera*, he launched on a bold experiment. He decided to publish the work himself and appointed carpenter and wood-engraver George Allen as his agent.

George Allen, Ruskin's very successful publisher from 1871 until his death in 1907.

Convinced that time would prove his new methods right, Ruskin gradually transferred all his books from his former publishers, Smith, Elder & Co, to George Allen, and by 1873 Allen had become the sole publisher, acting directly under Ruskin. Allen proved to be a good businessman. For many years he acted exclusively as Ruskin's publisher and during this period the sales of old and new titles alike soared.

Eventually Ruskin and Allen agreed that slight modification was needed to Ruskin's revolutionary sales scheme. The adapted method of publishing led to eventual changes in the book world and paved the way for the Net Book Agreement, which governed the way in which modern publishing and bookselling practice was controlled until the 1990s.

At the same time that Ruskin took charge of his own publishing he also greatly improved the style and appearance of his books. Hitherto the layout had been largely the responsibility of the publishers and many of his earlier books, particularly the smaller volumes such as *Time and Tide* and *The Political Economy of Art* represent all that was bad in mid-Victorian printing. The new format that he planned for Fors Clavigera, with better paper, wider margins, clearer typeface and better proportions, became the style on which all of his later books were

Ruskin's 'Time and Tide', published by Smith, Elder & Co in 1867; notice the poor arrangement of the type on the pages.

68   *The Storm-Cloud of*

opposite, on the right hand, the worship of the Golden Calf is symbolized by a single decorated pillar, with the calf on its summit, surrounded by the clouds and darkness of a furious storm, issuing from the mouths of fiends;—uprooting the trees, and throwing down the rocks, above the broken tables of the Law, of which the fragments lie in the foreground.

2. These conditions are mainly in the arrangement of the lower rain-clouds in flakes thin and detached enough to be illuminated by early or late sunbeams: their textures are then more softly blended than those of the upper cirri, and have the qualities of painted, instead of burnished or inflamed, colour.

They were thus described in the 4th chapter of the 7th part of 'Modern Painters':—

"Often in our English mornings, the rain-clouds in the dawn form soft level fields, which melt imperceptibly into the blue; or when of less extent, gather into apparent bars, crossing the sheets of broader cloud

the Nineteenth Century.   69

above; and all these bathed throughout in an unspeakable light of pure rose-colour, and purple, and amber, and blue, not shining, but misty-soft, the barred masses, when seen nearer, found to be woven in tresses of cloud, like floss silk, looking as if each knot were a little swathe or sheaf of lighted rain.

No clouds form such skies, none are so tender, various, inimitable; Turner himself never caught them. Correggio, putting out his whole strength, could have painted them, —no other man."

3. I did not, in writing this sentence, forget Mr. Gladstone's finely scholastic enthusiasm for Homer; nor Mr. Newton's for Athenian—(I wish it had not been also for Halicarnassian) sculpture. But Byron loved Greece herself—through her death—and *to* his own; while the subsequent refusal of England to give Greece one of our own princes for a king, has always been held by me the most ignoble, cowardly, and lamentable, of all our base commercial *im*policies.

'Storm-Cloud of the Nineteenth Century' illustrating Ruskin's influence on the improved layout of George Allen's 1884 edition.

based. Some of the lectures in the 1880s were printed in a larger format using larger type. *Storm-Cloud of the Nineteenth Century, In Montibus Sanctis* and others are, in feeling and appearance, the forerunners of the private-press movement which, some ten years later, was to lead to the much greater typographical awareness of today.

FORS CLAVIGERA AND ST GEORGE'S GUILD

Fors, like most of Ruskin's other books at this period, was published in monthly parts. The nature of the subject matter of Fors changed from issue to issue. As Ruskin continued his various crusades it provided him with the platform which he needed to keep his public up to date with his ideas and their practical outcome. One issue might deal with the evils of modern commercialism, the next would be autobiographical, the next packed with art criticism.

During the first year of *Fors Clavigera* Ruskin's campaign for the reform of England was crystallised in his original scheme to establish St George's Guild. He gave £7000, a tithe or tenth of his possessions, to the new scheme. (The remainder of his inheritance had gone on bad investments, works of art for himself and others, and various philanthropic ventures.) The objects of the Guild were 'to set the example of socialistic capital as opposed to a national debt, and of socialistic labour as opposed to competitive struggle for life'. Each member of the Guild was to do some form of work for his living and was to live by certain moral and religious principles laid down by Ruskin. He must also contribute a tithe of his income to the Guild funds. In turn the Guild was to buy land for the agricultural members to operate and mills and factories for the other members (where water power was to be used in preference to steam). The people employed would receive a fair wage and do healthy work and the Guild would supply places of recreation and instruction, schools and libraries. The 'Bibliotheca Pastorum', the Guild's library of books, was selected and edited by Ruskin and included Xenophon's *Economist*, Gotthelf's *Ulric the Farm Servant*, and *A Knight's Faith*, Ruskin's biography of Sir Herbert Edwardes. Ruskin was not planning to establish a commune; he was merely laying down certain ways in which Guild members should run communally owned industries and farms.

Although the Guild attracted a few Companions, the response was not great. Over the years, land was given or acquired at Barmouth in

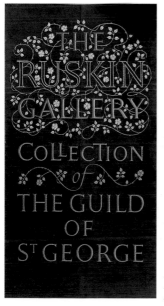

Wales, in the Lake District, in Yorkshire, at Bewdley in Worcestershire, at Westmill in Hertfordshire and at Sheffield. It was at Sheffield that Ruskin established the Guild's museum, stocking it largely from his own collection or pocket. He did not seek to create another typically Victorian museum of stuffed animals, fossils and a few poorly labelled archaeological specimens, but to provide a collection of beauty in all its forms. The Guild museum's collection was built up with Old Master paintings or good copies of them (he employed a whole team of copyists, some of them formerly in his Working Men's College class); there were some of his own drawings, illuminated manuscripts,

In 1985 the Guild of St George commissioned David Kindersley to design and cut this 120 by 60 cm tablet to stand at the entrance to its new gallery in Sheffield.

47

Ruskin met Rose La Touche in 1858. By 1861 he had fallen in love with her. She gradually became ill and died in 1875 aged just thirty-one. The tragedy of their love coloured much of the remainder of Ruskin's life and work. He made this portrait of her probably about 1866.

beautiful minerals and semi-precious stones, casts and photographs of fine sculpture and architecture, and a small but significant library of important literature and fine books. Henry Swan, a former Working Men's College pupil, was appointed its first curator and did much to interpret the significance of the various exhibits. The Guild's collection is still in Sheffield and has its own gallery in the city's Millennium Galleries. The Guild still functions today and aims to foster Ruskin's ideals. It sponsored a 'Campaign for Drawing', remembering that Ruskin believed 'that the greatest thing a human soul ever does in this world is to see something, and tell what it saw in a plain way'.

WHISTLER

Some of Ruskin's art criticism in *Fors* was to have repercussions. At the opening of the new Grosvenor Gallery in London in 1877 Ruskin saw a group of pictures by J. A. McN. Whistler. He considered them to be of poor workmanship and in *Fors* he wrote that 'their eccentricities are almost always in some degree forced, and their imperfections gratuitously, if not impertinently, indulged... the ill-educated conceit of the artist so nearly [approaches] the aspect of wilful imposture. I have seen, and heard, much of Cockney impudence before now;

WHISTLER · VERSUS · RUSKIN ·

AN APPEAL TO THE LAW.

NAUGHTY CRITIC, TO USE BAD LANGUAGE! SILLY PAINTER, TO GO TO LAW ABOUT IT!

The outcome of the Whistler versus Ruskin libel action, as seen by Edward Linley Sambourne in 'Punch', December 1878. The judge hands the farthing damages to Whistler, who is shown with his characteristic lock of white hair; he is said to have worn the coin on his watch-chain. Ruskin appears as an 'Old Pelican in the Art Wilderness' (the pelican is the crest of Corpus Christi College, Oxford, of which Ruskin was a Fellow).

but never expected to hear a coxcomb ask two hundred guineas for flinging a pot of paint in the public's face.' Not unnaturally the artist was upset, and he sued Ruskin for libel. It was almost a year before the case came to court and such was Ruskin's power as an art critic that during this period Whistler did not sell a single picture. The two-day hearing became a *cause célèbre*. Ruskin was found guilty; the court had no option but to find him so. But its feeling was reflected in the penalty it extracted. Ruskin had to pay one farthing damages and the costs were divided. Ruskin's costs were paid by his friends and admirers who opened a fund for the purpose as a token of their regard and respect. Whistler had to find his own £200 and within six months was bankrupt. The outcome may seem unfair to Whistler but Ruskin was not being vindictive in *Fors*; he was honestly following his self-appointed task of pointing out to the British public what he considered to be good and bad in art.

FEVER PITCH

The decade beginning about 1875 was perhaps the busiest period of Ruskin's life. For sheer industry he can rarely have been equalled. His British and continental tours continued. Frequently he took groups of friends with him and in addition to introducing them to his favourite haunts – Chamouni, Lucca, Florence, Venice – he maintained his regular correspondence of upwards of twenty letters daily; he received, corrected and returned proofs to his printers at Aylesbury; he wrote sometimes three or four books simultaneously, with monthly deadlines for the new parts; he sketched, and he assembled material for future work. At home, he lectured at Oxford and elsewhere; he planned,

arranged and catalogued collections of his own Turners, Prouts and Hunts for exhibition; he assembled collections of minerals (and wrote the catalogues) to be given to various schools. At Whitelands, a ladies' college in Chelsea, he was instrumental in beginning a May Queens ceremony, annually giving a specially designed and made gold cross and copies of his own books. The tradition continues at Whitelands (now a college of the University of Surrey Roehampton), the Guild of St George annually giving the Ruskin books.

For relaxation at Brantwood he

The author presenting the Ruskin books to Abigail Forder, the Whitelands May Queen of 2003.

Ruskin, billhook in hand, climbs one of his paths at Brantwood to bring another piece of moorland into use. A self-portrait silhouette of 1881.

rowed on the lake, chopped trees on his estate, enlarged his harbour, constructed reservoirs and waterfalls, and made excursions into the Lake District to places with childhood memories.

Proserpina, a book on 'wayside flowers', *Deucalion*, geological studies, *St Mark's Rest*, 'the history of Venice written for the help of the few travellers who still care for her monuments', *The Bible of Amiens*, the story of the cathedral and much else, and *Guide to the Principal Pictures in the Academy at Venice* all date from this period.

Finally, at the end of the decade he began his last book, *Praeterita: Outlines of Scenes and Thoughts perhaps worthy of memory in my past life*. His autobiography was planned on ambitious lines. It was to run to three volumes, each consisting of twelve parts. Large portions of parts one and two had already been printed in *Fors* and the first three parts were published in July 1885. Thereafter he kept to a regular monthly schedule until he was half-way through the second volume.

But the pace which Ruskin set himself in the 1870s and 1880s was too great. Overwork led to ill-health and a series of mental breakdowns and there were periods when he was too ill to work. He struggled on with *Praeterita* but by the time he had begun the third volume he knew that he would never complete his original plan. After the second part of that volume he leapt ahead in time and part three was largely devoted to Rose La Touche, a young lady with whom he had been in love and who had died in 1875. The final part, 'Joanna's Care', was published in July 1889. It was a tribute to Joan Severn, who had come into the family in 1864 to care for Margaret Ruskin, who had later nursed Ruskin through his illnesses, and who was to be his mainstay for the next eleven years.

Ruskin had walked in Siena with his American friend, Charles Eliot Norton. This image of the façade of the Duomo in Siena is from a daguerreotype in Ruskin's collection.

Ruskin remained a master of English prose to the end of his last book. '[We] walked together that evening on the hills above, where the fireflies among the scented thickets shone fitfully in the still undarkened air. *How* they shone! moving like fine-broken starlight through the purple leaves. How they shone! through the sunset that faded into thunderous night as I entered Siena three days before, the white edges of the mountainous clouds still lighted from the west, and the openly golden sky calm behind the gate of Siena's heart, with its still golden words, *Cor magis tibi Sena pandit*, and the fireflies everywhere in the sky and cloud rising and falling, mixed with the lightening, and more intense than the stars.'

Ruskin enjoyed rowing. Here he is, with Joan Severn, in his boat 'Jumping Jenny', which was built for him at Coniston in 1879.

The final years

REST

Ruskin was seventy in February 1889. A final illness in the summer left him incapable of further concentrated effort. He had written his last book, made his last sketch (of the Langdale Pikes on 3rd June). In the next eleven years he was to write only five more letters. His last attempt was a letter of condolence to Mary Gladstone on the death of her father. He rowed or was rowed on the lake; he walked a little and occasionally visited his near neighbours. His last visit to the village of Coniston was in 1893 when he attended the Choral Society's concert at which Joan Severn and her daughters were singing. Old friends visited him at Brantwood; some were admitted, others were not. The curious often wandered by in the hope of catching a glimpse of him.

John Ruskin outlived many of his contemporaries into the twentieth century. The winter of 1900 was a severe one and in January he caught influenza, dying on 20th January at Brantwood. A grave was offered in Westminster Abbey but was declined. 'There's no place like Coniston',

William Holman Hunt (right) visited Ruskin at Brantwood in September 1894 and they were photographed together by Frederick Hollyer.

he had said, and he was buried near his village friends in Coniston churchyard. His grave was marked by a tall cross of local stone, designed by W. G. Collingwood, and a year later a memorial was erected to his memory at Friar's Crag, overlooking Derwentwater, on a plot of land which was to become the National Trust's first Lake District property.

In a long and active life Ruskin had taught the dignity of labour and the brotherhood of man and had encouraged success through skill and hard work. His teaching was a

The author at Ruskin's grave on the centenary of his death, 20th January 1900, with the Guild of St George's wreath, cut from the same tree that G. F. Watts's wreath had come from a century earlier.

The Ruskin Galleries were built at Bembridge School in 1929 to house the Whitehouse Collection.

cross between socialism and communism and both Morris and Shaw followed his lead, as did all the early English socialists. Ruskin showed the way and many put his teaching to practical use.

INFLUENCE

After Ruskin took charge of his own publishing in the 1870s, sales of his books increased enormously, and with this greater exposure of his writings came a much broader interest in him and appreciation of his words. Throughout the 1870s and 1880s he was a regular correspondent with the press. Reports of his activities and his health featured in the press, and he frequently appeared as the caricaturists' subject.

Ruskin Societies proliferated. The first was founded in Manchester in 1878; by 1900, when the Newport, Isle of Wight, society was established, there were a dozen societies holding regular meetings to hear lectures on Ruskin subjects, or to read and discuss his books.

Inspired by his teaching, several co-operative communities were established in North America. For a short while, the most flourishing was the little town of Ruskin, Tennessee. In the late 1890s there was a thriving community of some 250 inhabitants, with printers, a chewing-gum manufactory, and a 'leather-suspender' factory. Another little colony called Ruskin in Canada was based on a flourishing sawmill.

The Ruskin Art Club of Los Angeles was founded in 1888, initially to study art, and is now the oldest ladies' club in the city. There was a Ruskin Club in Boston. Trenton, Missouri, had its Ruskin College

(1900) with courses to study industrial economy, a social-science-oriented liberal arts course, and a business course.

In *Fors Clavigera* Ruskin had promoted the education of the working man and, to honour his name, the first extramural college in Britain, Ruskin College, Oxford, was established in 1899 'in order to bring an education worthy of a citizen to the door of every man and woman'. Other educational establishments were Ruskin Hall at Birkenhead, and the Ruskin School Home (1900) in Norfolk, where 'we will take for our basis John Ruskin's educational idea'.

Arts and Crafts movements, influenced by his teaching, flourished in Britain and the United States, and the Lake District's own Arts and Crafts movement existed largely because of Ruskin's presence in the area.

Essentially Ruskin was an impractical man. He threw out ideas and left it to others to put them into practice. Even Companions giving property to the Guild of St George were expected to administer it themselves along Ruskinian lines. Ruskin had warned of the dangers of atmospheric pollution in his lectures *The Storm-Cloud of the Nineteenth Century* and had advocated smokeless zones and green belts around cities. Eventually his warnings were heeded with the Clean Air Act. His housing experiments had been based on fair rents and security of tenure; eventually we had the Rent Restrictions Act.

Octavia Hill, who had managed his London property and come under his influence from the 1850s, and Hardwick Rawnsley, who had been

an undergraduate at Oxford when Ruskin was Slade Professor, together with Robert Hunter, founded the National Trust. Thus they put into practice Ruskin's proposal that the country should have a National Store rather than a National Debt.

It was left to philanthropists and later politicians to implement Ruskin's desire to see free schools and libraries. When the first large group of Labour members was

The Ruskin Memorial at Friar's Crag, Derwentwater, was unveiled on 6th October 1900 by Joan Severn. Canon Hardwick Rawnsley was responsible for the fund-raising, and the plot became the National Trust's first Lake District property.

Ryuzo Mikimoto (left) showing part of his collection to Professor Masami Kimura.

elected to Parliament in 1906, the *Review of Reviews* asked them to name the authors who had most influenced them. Forty-five of them responded; the author at the head of the list, with seventeen members acknowledging their debt, was Ruskin. One of these 1906 politicians was J. Ramsay MacDonald, whose copy of the Doves Press edition of *Unto This Last* now stands on the present author's shelves. He was to become Britain's Labour Prime Minister in 1924.

Further afield, in France Marcel Proust translated *The Bible of Amiens* and *Sesame and Lilies*. Mahatma Gandhi read *Unto This Last* and later said that it had changed his whole way of life. In Russia, Tolstoy had a great admiration for Ruskin's writings. In Japan Ryuzo Mikimoto, who inherited the cultured-pearl industry developed by his father, devoted his life to bringing Ruskin's ideas to his fellow countrymen by translating many of Ruskin's books into Japanese and opening a Ruskin Library in Tokyo.

Ruskin's influence has been both important and international. For more than half a century after his death, interest in him was at a very low ebb, but the pendulum has swung, and Ruskin's influence on our way of life and thought is once again appreciated. Each year many thousands of people visit his home at Brantwood, while scholars from around the world carry out study and research in the Ruskin Library at Lancaster University.

Principal events

1819	John Ruskin born on 8th February in London; Queen Victoria born
1824	First visit to Lake District and Scotland
1825	First visit to Continent
1829	First poem published in *The Spiritual Times*
1830	Tour of Lake District; writes *Iteriad*
1831	Begins drawing lessons with Runciman
1832	Receives gift of Rogers's *Italy*
1833	Tour to Germany, Switzerland and Italy
1834	Begins watercolour lessons with Copley Fielding
1835	First long continental tour
1837	Enters Christ Church, Oxford; writes *Poetry of Architecture*; Queen Victoria ascends throne
1839	Begins to collect Turner watercolours; wins Newdigate Prize at Oxford; meets Wordsworth
1841	End of early drawing style; writes *The King of the Golden River*
1843	Takes MA degree; publishes *Modern Painters* I
1845	First tour to France, Switzerland and Italy without his parents
1846	*Modern Painters* II
1848	Marries Effie Gray; tour to Normandy
1849	*Seven Lamps of Architecture*; long visit to Venice
1850	Collected *Poems* published
1851	*Stones of Venice* I; defence of Pre-Raphaelites begins; long visit to Venice
1853	*Stones of Venice* II and III; writes *Lectures on Architecture and Painting* at Glenfinlas
1854	Marriage annulled; foundation of Working Men's College; Academy Notes annually until 1859
1856	*Modern Painters* III and IV; at work on Oxford Museum
1857	*Political Economy of Art; Elements of Drawing*; arranged Turner Bequest
1858	Meets Rose La Touche
1859	Visits Winnington Hall School; *The Two Paths*
1860	*Modern Painters* V; *Unto This Last* in *Cornhill Magazine*
1861	Presents Turner collections to Oxford and Cambridge
1862	'Essays on Political Economy' in *Fraser's Magazine*
1864	Death of J. J. Ruskin; buys property in Marylebone for housing experiment; cousin Joan Agnew enters household
1865	*Sesame and Lilies*
1866	*Ethics of the Dust; Crown of Wild Olive*
1868	Long visit to northern France
1869	*Flamboyant Architecture of the Somme; Queen of the Air*; appointed Slade Professor of Fine Art at Oxford
1870	*Lectures on Art*

1871   Illness at Matlock; buys Brantwood; endows Oxford Drawing
        Mastership; starts Guild of St George; street sweeping experiment;
        death of Margaret Ruskin; Joan Agnew marries Arthur Severn;
        undertakes own publishing; *Fors Clavigera* begins
1874   Hinksey diggings; opens tea shop
1875   *Proserpina; Deucalion; Academy Notes*; death of Rose La Touche;
        founds Guild of St George Museum
1876   Long visit to Venice
1877   *Guide to the Academy at Venice; St Mark's Rest*
1878   Whistler v. Ruskin libel action; arranged Turner exhibition at Fine
        Art Society
1879   Resigns Slade Professorship
1880   *Bible of Amiens*
1883   Resumes Slade Professorship; *The Art of England*
1885   *Praeterita* begins; resigns Slade Professorship
1888   Last tour of France, Switzerland and Italy
1889   *Praeterita* concluded; end of all literary and artistic work
1900   John Ruskin dies at Brantwood, 20th January
1901   Queen Victoria dies

*Ruskin copied this group of roses (below) from the dress
of Flora in Botticelli's painting 'Primavera' in 1874.
He later copied it on to a wood-block (left) and it was
engraved by Arthur Burgess for use on the title pages of
his later books.*

Bibliography

There have been many biographies and critical studies of John Ruskin. The first major biography, and still one of the best and most sympathetic, is *The Life and Work of John Ruskin*, in two volumes, by W. G. Collingwood (Methuen, 1893). This was rewritten as a single volume and the first of many editions was published in 1900. Another early standard biography is *The Life of John Ruskin*, in two volumes, by E. T. Cook (George Allen, 1911). Undoubtedly the most complete biography is *John Ruskin* by Tim Hilton (Yale University Press, two volumes, 1985–2000; one composite volume, 2002). Other works include:

Batchelor, J. *John Ruskin, No Wealth but Life*. Chatto & Windus, 2000.
Bell, Q. *Ruskin*. Oliver & Boyd, 1963; several reprints and translations.
Birkenhead, S. *Illustrious Friends*. Hamish Hamilton, 1965.
Brooks, M. W. *John Ruskin and Victorian Architecture*. Rutgers University Press, 1987.
Dearden, J. S. *John Ruskin, A Life in Pictures*. Sheffield University Press, 1999.
Hewison, R. *John Ruskin, The Argument of the Eye*. Thames & Hudson, 1976.
Hewison, R.; Warrell, I.; and Wildman, *S. Ruskin, Turner and the Pre-Raphaelites*. Tate Gallery, 2000.
Leon, D. *Ruskin, the Great Victorian*. Routledge, 1949; reprinted 1969.
Rosenberg, J. D. *The Darkening Glass, A Portrait of Ruskin's Genius*. Columbia University Press, 1961.
Viljoen, H. G. *Ruskin's Scottish Heritage*. University of Illinois Press, 1956.
Walton, P. *The Drawings of John Ruskin*. Clarendon Press, 1972; reprints.
Walton, P. *Master Drawings by John Ruskin*. Pilkington Press, 2000.

The standard edition of Ruskin's own writings is *The Library Edition of the Works of John Ruskin*, in thirty-nine volumes (George Allen, 1903–12; CD-ROM Cambridge University Press, 1996). Most of Ruskin's books went through many editions, particularly those published by George Allen, and these are usually available in second-hand bookshops. Useful volumes of selections or recent editions include:

Barrie, D. (editor). *Modern Painters*. André Deutsch, 1987; Pilkington Press, 2000.
Birch, D. (editor). *Fors Clavigera*. Whitehouse Series, Edinburgh University Press, 2000.

Burd, V. A. (editor). *The Ruskin Family Letters 1801–1843* (two volumes). Cornell University Press, 1973.

Clark, K. (editor). *Ruskin Today*. Murray, 1964, and many reprints.

Cockshut, A. O. J. (editor). *Praeterita*. Whitehouse Series, Ryburn, 1994.

Dearden, J. S. (editor). *A Tour to the Lakes in Cumberland. John Ruskin's Diary for 1830*. Scolar, 1990.

Dearden, J. S. (editor). *King of the Golden River*. Coach House Publications, 1999.

Evans, J., and Whitehouse, J. H. (editors). *The Diaries of John Ruskin* (three volumes). Clarendon Press, 1956–9.

Links, J. G. (editor). *The Stones of Venice*. Collins, 1960, and reprints.

Rosenberg, J. D. (editor). *The Genius of John Ruskin*. Allen & Unwin, 1964, and reprints.

Tucker, Paul (editor): *John Ruskin's "Resume" of Italian Art and Architecture* (1845). Sculoa Normale Superiore, Pisa, 2003.

Viljoen, H. G. (editor). *The Brantwood Diary of John Ruskin*. Yale University Press, 1971.

Chamouni, Aiguille Charmoz from the window of the 'Union', 1849. Ruskin considered that one of his principal contributions to art was his knowledge of geology. His father wrote of his son: 'From boyhood he has been an artist, but he has been a geologist from infancy, and his geology is perhaps now the best part of his Art, for it enables him to place before us rocks and mountains as they are in Nature, in place of the very bad likenesses of these objects presented to us in most of the old paintings or modern drawings'.

Where to see Ruskin

The principal collection of Ruskin material is that formed by the late J. Howard Whitehouse. This is now preserved at Brantwood, which he bought and established as an international memorial to Ruskin, and at the Ruskin Library, Lancaster University (Lancaster LA1 4YH; telephone 01524 593587; website: lancs.ac.uk/users/ruskinlib).

Whitehouse, who collected throughout the first half of the twentieth century, was buying at a time when there was very little interest in Ruskin. He was thus able to bring together a collection of many hundreds of drawings by Ruskin and his circle, his diaries, a substantial number of his notebooks, manuscripts of many of his books, and thousands of his letters. He also acquired many books from Ruskin's own library and built up a substantial collection of books by and about Ruskin.

Brantwood (Coniston, Cumbria LA21 8AD; telephone: 01539 441396; website: www.brantwood.org.uk), Ruskin's home for the final twenty-eight years of his life, was bought by Whitehouse in 1932 and, with the exception of the war years, has been open to the public ever since. It is situated on the quiet, east side of Coniston Lake. Here the visitor can see more pictures by Ruskin and his friends. Much of Ruskin's dining room, study and drawing room furniture has been reassembled in the house. His carriage and boat are preserved in the coach-house. On the 250 acre (100 hectare) estate, the gardens have been restored to what they were in Ruskin's time. The Moorland Garden is the site of Ruskin's visionary experiment in upland agriculture; the Professor's Garden, which he planned and managed, was used for growing flowers, fruit, herbs and vegetables suitable for a cottager's garden; his Zig-zaggy Garden was inspired by Dante's Divine Comedy. Meanwhile the Harbour Walk and the High Walk, with their spring flowers, azaleas, rhododendrons and other rare shrubs and trees, were the work of Joan Severn.

Anyone interested in Ruskin and his work ought to visit the house and grounds at Brantwood. While at Coniston, the visitor should not miss the Ruskin Museum, which originally grew out of Ruskin's generosity to the village (The Ruskin Museum, Coniston, Cumbria LA21 8DU; telephone: 01539 441164; website: www.ruskinmuseum.com). Here are more drawings, letters and other interesting relics, together with local material. Ruskin's grave, marked by a tall cross designed by W. G. Collingwood, is in the churchyard. The east window of the Catholic church was given by Ruskin and here also are some miniatures, cut and given from one of his medieval manuscripts.

Other collections of his drawings may be seen in:

Ashmolean Museum, Beaumont Street, Oxford OX1 2PH. Telephone: 01865 278000. Website: www.ashmolean.org   (The Ruskin Drawing School collection.)

The British Museum, Great Russell Street, London WC1B 3DG. Telephone: 020 7323 8000. Website: www.britishmuseum.org

Ruskin Gallery, Millennium Galleries, Arundel Gate, Sheffield S1 2PP. Telephone: 0114 278 2600. Website: www.sheffieldgalleries.org.uk (The Collection of

the Guild of St George.)
South London Gallery, 65 Peckham Road, London SE5 8UH. Telephone: 020 7703 6120. Website: www.southlondongallery.org

There are other important groups of literary material in:
UNITED KINGDOM
Bodleian Library, Broad Street, Oxford OX1 3BG. Telephone: 01865 277216. Website: www.bodley.ox.ac.uk
The British Library, 96 Euston Road, London NW1 2DB. Telephone: 0870 444 1500. Website: www.bl.uk
The John Rylands University Library of Manchester, Oxford Road, Manchester M13 9PP. Telephone: 0161 275 3751. Website: www.library.manchester.ac.uk

UNITED STATES
Beinecke Library (at Yale University), 121 Wall Street, New Haven, Connecticut 06511. Telephone: (001) 203 432 2977. Website: www.library.yale.edu/ beinecke
Columbia University Libraries, 535 North 114th Street, New York NY 10027. Telephone: (001) 212 854 2271. Website: www.columbia.edu/cu/lweb
The Huntington Library, 1151 Oxford Road, San Marino CA 91108. Telephone: (001) 626 405 2100. Website: www.huntington.org
The Morgan Library and Museum, 225 Madison Avenue on 36th Street, New York, NY 10016. Telephone: 212 685 0008. Website: www.themorgan.org

JAPAN
Ruskin Library, 2-15-15 Tsukiji, Chuo-ku, Tokyo 140-0045. Website: www.ruskintoday.org/tokyo.htm (The Mikimoto Collection)

Brantwood today. The original cottage may be identified in the centre of the building. The house was gradually enlarged by Ruskin principally to accommodate the Severns, who shared it with him.

Index